RECONN HEARTS: OVERCOMING RELATIONSHIP CRISES

HOW TO REORGANIZE YOUR MIND
AND
BUILD TOGETHER THE WAY TO HAPPINESS

MELISSA HERNÁNDEZ-JACZEWSKA

Publisher

BookEdit

512 087 075
e-mail: redakcja@bookedit.pl
www.bookedit.pl
facebook.pl/BookEdit/
instagram.com/BookEdit/

CHAPTERS

FROM THE AUTHOR'S NOTEBOOK

Life consists of stages – January 2023

Stages have different durations.

Sometimes they seem endless, other times they slip out of our hands.

Some stages are difficult and tedious, other can be magical. They all come to an end sometime. All of them.

The end of one heralds the beginning of a new one. That means change. Sometimes almost imperceptible, and sometimes radical.

In the twists and turns we face in life, we can choose to suffer for what we have left behind. However, we have the ability to keep positive experiences in our mind and soul, and to think back to those events as many times as we need to.

We have the ability to open the door to what is coming.

We can live in the past or learn to let go.

As I write this, I relive in my mind all the cravings I fulfilled during my last days in Mexico. I am thankful for them. I thank all the people who made these wonderful days possible. But they are over for now.

Half asleep and awake, sitting in a large hall at the airport in Paris, waiting for my flight to Warsaw. I still have my head in the clouds. Watching people pass by. What stories have just ended and which are about to begin? What or who did they say goodbye to?

What or who will they find again? Everything is in constant motion.

I review the 46 years I left behind.

The turns of my life. All the hard times and adversities. Sincere smiles that fill the afternoons. Various landscapes. Deafening fatigue. Concerns, achievements.

Love.

I immerse myself in memories, think about the trips I took, lazy mornings. About all those sunny days with music. About those when it rained causing floods.

I am thinking about the range of colors, their intensity. From A to Z.

I take a deep breath, smile and thank God for another year of my life and for the fact that he still makes me come across valuable people with whom I can share what I have and whom I can trust. I have someone to learn from and someone to teach.

They say that the most important thing is not the road, but who you walk along it with.

I feel thankful to life for teaching me to let go. Reorganize. To be like water that adapts to the shape of a glass. And when I have no limits, no barriers, I reinvent myself.

And when I forget what I've learned, I learn again. I keep in mind that life consists of episodes, stages and constant changes. I have the impression that then a person enjoys everything – with even greater intensity.

This segment has ended.

I brought the sun with me in a suitcase, lots of hugs and love. I took all I could from the interesting conversations with my parents and celebrations with friends. I brought with me living by the beach, palm trees and all those delicious meals eaten with people close to me.

I don't know what left those I met with, but I still recall the positive energy generated during these meetings.

I'm going back home.

To build new stories. Live in the present. To spread the beauty, I acquired there.

I feel that this year will bring new, magical surprises! Let it be that way!

INTRODUCTION

This book was written with the intention of motivating you, dear readers, to break free from the passivity of everyday life. See who you really are, what is the purpose of your life – both personal and professional. With the intention that you become aware of your actions, your attitudes and your emotions, which you use without reason every day, obtaining results that are sometimes unsatisfactory for yourself. By getting used to observing our behavior and emotions we can make the conscious decision to continue using these patterns that we have been acquiring sometimes from a very early age and we repeat automatically as if it were the only way to function. Live your life to its fullest potential.

On the way to create a relationship that will give you full love, happiness and satisfaction.

You will find some of the most common issues that I attend to in my work as a psychologist, both in individual and couple therapy, as well as questions and exercises that will help you make the decision to sufficient changes to have a better relationship with yourself and with your loved one. To have a more harmonious, balanced and happy life.

In this book you will find excerpts from my personal notebook. I chose to include them to illustrate the different nuances of certain emotional states that I experienced myself. These are very deep chapters of my life that I would like to share with you. I wonder with which of them you will identify yourself!

I would like this book, despite the fact that the direct content is addressed to heterosexual people, to be intended for all those who love – the whole, beautiful LGBTQ+ rainbow.

Love is love

The relationships, mechanisms and stereotypes from which we come from, by which we were involuntarily formed, they are part of your past, they represent years of your life, childhood and adolescence. For some reason you learned to behave that way, but it is time to step away from some of those patterns, make a decision and embrace the present as an adult. I hope that this publication will become a driving force to start a dialogue with yourself. It will make you autonomous, aware, which will translate into an increase of your self-esteem.

Travel through these pages to allow yourself to know your partner, where you will once again immerse yourself in their needs and dreams with greater attention. Create your destiny on your own terms, respecting yourself, your surroundings and your own values.

Treat this reading as a journey into the depths of a stormy ocean. Don't be afraid to lose yourself in its great blue, but remember to emerge from time to time, lay your back on its surface and look at the sky. Breathe.

Compare the content you find here to your experience over the years. Create goals, change existing standards. Go with the flow, but don't treat it as a task you have to finish as soon as possible, tick off and throw into the abyss.

Allow yourself to take a slow intellectual and emotional walk, as in the case of your new favorite TV series, which surprises you every now and then, tying you to it permanently.

It is a great honor for me that you are reaching for this book. From now on, we will not run away from the rain, we will start dancing together in it.

Don't wait for the storm to pass, learn to dance in the rain

ABOUT THE AUTHOR

I come from the rich in history and culture, Mexico. There I gradu-
ated with honors from the Faculty of Psychology at the Universi-
dad de Las Americas in Puebla.

I have been living in Poland since 2001, where I nostrified
my diploma at the University of Warsaw.

I specialize in short and long-term therapies, in which I address the problems of civilization diseases that generate anxiety, stress, and low self-esteem, often defined as depression.

I derive the greatest successes and professional satisfaction from working with couples, often from different countries and backgrounds. More than 15 years of practice in solving problems of everyday life in relationships resulted in writing this book. The solutions developed over the years now have a chance to reach the general public, often also those who have limited access to a psychologist or do not have the resources for full-time therapy in a clinic.

Our first teachers are our parents, we observe their experiences in the husband-wife relationship, and how a relationship should and should not look like. This is knowledge that is worth collecting and using in your own emotional life.

I was lucky enough to grow up in a loving home where my parents have been inextricably connected for fifty years. Their relationship, although stable, went through many crises. However, both mom and dad taught me to get up from every fall and become stronger and wiser for the future.

Privately, I am a warm, open person who loves people and dancing.

None of us should claim to be an expert when it comes to relationships. Every theory needs to be reflected in practice. In my case, marriage to a Pole, which required and will require us to work due to differences in characters, cultural identity and the fact that we come from different worlds, gives me a wealth of experience that I use in my work with patients.

Ultimately, it is thanks to our own knowledge and intuition that we build with my husband a common path to happiness.

That is what I wish for you, dear readers!

Melissa Hernández-Jaczewska

PART I

"ME"

A FEW WORDS ABOUT LOVE

It is safe to say that our life is incomplete without love. Love makes us feel happy, lets us accept ourselves fully, as we get to understand the behaviors and needs of others. Love is a bright and pure energy. However, without working on self-love, returning to one's own "*ME* ", taking care of and accepting one's flaws, because we all have them, even the most promising relationship has no chance of development, let alone full happiness.

It is important to be aware that the most important person in your life is not your partner, child or mother, but you. Meanwhile, it is normal in our everyday life that we are our own greatest censors and critics.

Doesn't that sound terrifying?

When was the last time you did something for yourself that was an impulse of pleasure?

When was the last time you took care of yourself to such an extent that you silenced intrusive thoughts and focused only on what is here and now?

Remember to appreciate yourselves not only on holidays, allow ourselves to make mistakes. Do not criticize ourselves at every step! Mistakes happen – what's more – they have to happen to us. Every day we struggle with a huge number of tasks and responsibilities, which are often accompanied by stress and anxiety about the thought of tomorrow. Several times a day we are exposed to bad news, outbursts of anger from loved ones and strangers, often unjustified.

Work on not dwelling on them, don't worry about them.

Start appreciating the little things – the beautiful weather, the smile of a stranger in the elevator, a good dinner prepared by a friend or partner. By appreciating the individual elements of life, we build happiness in all its aspects.

Because life consists of little moments, and ultimately it is them and the emotions associated with them that we remember and reminisce for years. Try to apply this principle to thinking about yourself. Look at yourself more often through the perspective of advantages.

Love is one of the most desirable feelings on the map of emotions.

Interestingly, according to medical terminology, there is no single, correct definition of love. Usually, we feel love for another person with whom we have a strong bond, and it is complemented by desire that we feel for them. Most often it wakes up unexpectedly and suddenly.

True love between two people is equal to mutual acceptance, support, trust, security and understanding. Its foundation is overcoming obstacles together along the way, which, as in life, requires many sacrifices, compromises, difficult conversations and forgiveness.

Love is a positive feeling that motivates you to change for the better. It gives energy for action, in which we develop, take on new challenges, and overcome depression, problems and even addictions. Its power gives us wings, thanks to which we look positively into the future.

American psychiatrist and one of the world's most popular researchers of love, Robert Stenberg*, in his many years of scientific work, has identified three components that love consists of;

1. Intimacy

It appears between people who become close and like to spend time together. In addition, they share and exchange information that allows them to meet their partner's needs. Understanding and tolerance for the shortcomings of both sides allows you to build a solid foundation for the relationship. Many theorists in the field of psychology and psychiatry recognize intimacy as the most important component of a relationship.

2. Passion

It is the feeling of excitement and strong sexual arousal that another person causes in us. It is associated with the absolute adoration of the object of desire and its idealization. Interestingly, passion also manifests itself in the mental sphere when we desire the presence of a partner. We miss them; we want to be with them.

* **Robert J. Sternberg** (born December 8, 1949). An American psychologist and psychometrician, Professor of Human Development at Cornell University.

3. Commitment

A component of the most rational part of love. It is what makes us fight for the relationship when the first cracks and problems appear. Depending on the degree of closeness and intimacy, being aware of communication gaps and troubles, we decide to work on the relationship. Moreover, we redefine our boundaries.

The ability to determine and guard them is a task that we may not necessarily like but we must upkeep. We are connected with them as with a partner – for life.

With different pressures or sometimes a single influence of the components on the partner, intimacy, passion and commitment – accompany us from the beginning throughout the development of the relationship and its whole duration. We can call a relationship complete only when the strongest phase – desire – is in its expiration. Then the intimacy and commitment between the partners are strengthened. Such love is preferred and most strived for all their lives by many people.

Most conscious partners undertake hard work to succeed in a long-term relationship while maintaining mutual desire. Knowing and meeting the needs of the other half protects the relationship from experimenting outside of it.

For most couples on earth, fidelity is still the most important thing, which in recent times has experienced a renaissance of importance.

The durability of the relationship is influenced by a strong intellectual bond and the implementation of the same or complementary passions. This fact was additionally strengthened in us by the recent COVID-19 coronavirus pandemic. Common interests and healthy competition make the partnership a challenge for us, which ultimately affects their attractiveness.

Most of us are aware that true love is not easy to achieve, but also … to feel.

It comes in different types and on many levels. Like most people, you can say that you are loved because your family, parents or grandparents show concern for you. The word – *"Love"* – is short but one of the most powerful words in our emotional vocabulary. It protects, but also exposes to suffering, brings people closer and frees them to start their own journey. In some marginal cases, throwing you into the abyss of pain and suffering. Love is the only higher emotion which power is able to manipulate an individual, regardless of their experience and strength of character. There are no strong ones when it comes to love, when it starts its work in our body, you can give in to it or fight a senseless fight with it. Regardless of your age, every moment is good to rebuild or build a new relationship based on understanding, mutual care and a sense of security.

For love it's worth it, always.

THE PERFECT RELATIONSHIP.
IS THERE ONE?

This is a question that we all ask ourselves. By carefully observing the couples around us, we are rarely able to say for sure — yes, they are perfect for each other. Because being perfect is not about being happy all the time in a relationship. Thinking about mankind, we exclude this idealistic image.

Let's forget once and for all that anything in life can be perfect and remember everything and everyone has flaws.

Let's focus on ourselves, what makes us believe that a relationship is perfect when we think about it? No problems, no arguments, stable financial situation? Or maybe gifts from a loved one or invitations to exotic trips? Mistake.

A relationship is a complicated matter, which is built by two independent individuals, putting a lot of energy into it – work, sacrifices, negotiations and emotions. When entering any relationship, we should think about building it from the start. This includes an element of effort and pushing the boundaries of comfort. That is why it is so important to enter into relationships consciously, with the energy of action and the desire to change for the better.

There are cases in which numerous failures in finding a partner for us make our expectations towards the next ones grow exponentially. Our attitude towards the world and people is also changing. By looking for the ideal, we become difficult and demanding in the unattractive sense of the word:

- *"I will never meet someone perfect for me".*
- *"This relationship will end in a fiasco again".*
- *"I'm not fit to be in a relationship".*

Often, knowing that your search does not bring results, you look for an alternative, making the mistake of getting involved with the wrong person.

Think about what kind of a partner will give you love, a sense of security and you will be happy with.

Humans evolve throughout life; we must be cautious of the changes that occur in and around us. Approach relationships logically and pragmatically, save your heart and pelvic impulses for romance. Be mindful when entering a relationship.

Frequent conversations, a sober look at your partner – forget about rose-colored glasses – a comparison of your values, goals and ambitions will show if you are made for each other. Matching is extremely important to the happiness and success of a relationship.

It is important that you bond with a person, and not with the image of your idealized expectations. This will give the feeling that you are in the right place for your future.

NO SELF-LOVE

Just reading this phrase makes me sad.

This is one of the most common issues I encounter in my practice. How do I want to distribute love to others if I have not learned to love myself? To respect myself. To take into account my own needs. To talk to myself in a kind manner.

More and more of us have a problem with self-acceptance, liking ourselves, let alone loving ourselves. This fact most often results from all kinds of problems and difficulties as well as routines that accumulated in childhood and adolescence, penetrate into our current life. If as a child you suffered harm, lack of acceptance, you had to fight for attention – the natural state of affairs is a problem with the interpretation of love and its mechanisms. This translates into the harmony and balance in your future relationships, not only romantic ones.

Low self-esteem makes us doubt our partner's good intentions, the quality and intensity of their feelings. Such thinking is a trap we have built for ourselves over the years. A wounded psyche that we have not worked on and are not currently working on can make us close ourselves from the outside world and others, falling into a spiral of negative thoughts and actions.

Nowadays, when life is speeding faster and faster, and we are overwhelmed with a huge number of tasks, duties, restrictions and information, we escape into time fillers to relax. Giving in to them leads to automatic, thoughtless actions. We have little time left to think about ourselves, to respond to our needs, thoughts and desires.

We often forget to slow down from the daily rush and ask ourselves important questions:

- *"Wait a minute, is this what I really want?"*
- *"What do I like to do for myself?"*
- *"Am I taking good care of myself?"*

Pay attention to how you answer these questions, they will tell you if you are meeting your main need – *"self-love"*.

These types of questions should give you an idea of how much attention you pay to yourself on a daily basis. Have you started treating yourself as the most important person in the whole world? Is that the case with you? Stop for a moment, what is your self-image?

How often do we think and talk badly about ourselves? In many cases, we believe ourselves to be weak, pathetic, not smart enough or not attractive enough.

- *It seems impossible to love us.*
- *We don't deserve a better tomorrow.*
- *We are not attractive or thin enough.*

Such a negative image of ourselves, which we pass on to others, will not make the world love us more than ourselves...

If you have at least half of the negative self-image I have presented to you, it's high time for a change!

Don't treat yourself worse than others. Look for virtues in yourself, think of yourself only through their perspective. When you think of yourself in the wrong context, you project that kind of feeling onto those around you, who may therefore treat you in ways you don't deserve.

Example: When Monika was 14, her mother directly, in what she considered a joking tone, said: *"First your nose comes in the room, then you"*: From that moment, Monica hears the mocking comment from her mother, it comes back to her, which is why she cannot get rid of the complex weighing on her.

Today Monica is a successful adult who in her field has accomplished her goals, one after other. However, she still has a complex and asks everyone if she has a big nose. Despite the negative answers to her question, which logically should eliminate her complex, this does not happen. She doesn't believe their answers, and the first she sees in the mirror is still her nose and then the rest.

One of the reasons why we cannot release the opinions of others is because we concentrate on wanting to decipher other's intentions. Monica doesn't know if her mom wanted her to accept her nose using a constant joke, if she wanted to criticize her or if she had not any particular intention. The crucial matter is that such comments – "*you have legs like sticks*", "*you look like an elephant*" or "*short comings*" can hurt and remind you of themselves all your life. It is interesting that no matter that we listen to different kind of comments and opinions about our person, very often we decide to keep in mind those which are hurtful. Those comments get stuck into our physique and determinate what we think about ourselves for years and look at ourselves through that prism. The task for us is to shake ourselves out of similar, erroneous thinking and realize that we have left being hurt too much already from those comments and that it's time to start reorganizing what we think about ourselves today.

Example: Reflect on the last time you went to the supermarket. The shelves were full of items, but you only bought some of them, those that were needed. Perhaps looked at some items for a few minutes, sometimes had them in your hand but made the decision if you want to take them home, store them in the fridge and make them part of a meal.

So, if you are able to be selective about the products you buy, don't you think selecting the words that you usually use to describe yourself would also be a good idea? And those which you don't need just leave them at the "*store*"?

Exercise

Repeat this reflection every time you go to the supermarket and become aware that you are the one who decides what to take home and what not. Begin to observe what you keep in your mind, what opinions about yourself you have been carrying, how you have rated yourself.

Negative opinions and adjectives have impaired your definition of yourself for years or decades, hindered your development and hurt you already enough. On many occasions you no longer hear them in your present life, however you have kept them in your mental shopping cart, you have bought them and constantly carry them with you. Wake up and go to sleep with them, and next day you take them to your table and eat breakfast with them and the worst thing – you believed them!

As if every time you go to the supermarket you buy rotten fruit that you know is going to be bad for you, but you buy it anyway and eat it every day. It's like having a permanent tattoo on your skin.

So, do you think you're ready to stop buying that rotten fruit? To find how to remove those mental tattoos?

Exercise

Choose how to rate yourself. First choose 5 qualities that describe you. Then another 5. Maybe at first, it's hard for you because you're not used to seeing your positive and bright side. But reflect and write these positive aspects about yourself. Stick this paper in a place where you will see it constantly and start saving this new image of you in your mental shopping cart.

**Life is like a sine wave. We have good times
and bad times during its course.**

We alternately feel happy, satisfied, full of energy, so that times can come for nostalgia, melancholy or troubles. Accepting these states, agreeing to this balance, we gain a new, refreshed approach to life. The line of our existence is not flat, it resembles one from vitals monitors that show the beat of the heart.

Give yourself time to laugh, relax, walk in the clouds, lie down without much sense, but also scream, regret and cry. Humans are a highly complex being, charged, and mostly over-loaded with stimuli, bad information, moods of the surrounding environment – such a complicated machine must have a chance to relieve, regenerate and renew.

Exercise

Think about how you react to a mistake or mishap made by a loved one. Is it normal for you to be more understanding of your partner, friend or family than you are of yourself?

If so, start treating yourself like your best friend. Take comfort and, most importantly, forgive yourself.

In case you fail at something, you "*slip up*" talk to yourself the way you communicate with a friend. Soon you will see how your own healthy approach to yourself will translate into happiness!

CHARGING INTERNAL BATTERIES

One of the greatest dangers of modern civilization that threaten us is the fact that we are used to living in a fast pace. We require ourselves to be active and fully engaged seven days a week, downplaying the importance of rest, even thinking that it is reserved for lazy or weak individuals.

In the end, we forget about the most important person on earth, who we should care for and treat with tenderness and delicacy – I am talking about ourselves.

If we forget about it and let our body be taken over by tension and stress, we will reap their grim harvest for years. The feeling of stress is read by our body as a reaction that threatens us – physically and mentally. Most often it manifests itself in numerous body tensions, feeling of nausea and weakness, not allowing us to regenerate during sleep.

Ultimately, we are less effective at the tasks that each new day throws at us. Remember to keep an eye on your internal battery, recharge it as soon as you feel its level drop. Don't wait until you cross the thin red line where professional help is required.

Listen to your body, think about how often you feel tired, irritated, inpatient, can you focus on one thing alone?

Your body is sending you a signal – *"take care of me!"*

What's the best way to take care of your internal battery?

- Get some sleep.
- Go to a forest where you can *"lose yourself"* in the wilderness, breathe fresh air, find a connection with nature.
- Get up 15 minutes before your scheduled time and stretch your muscles after sleeping. Take a cool shower. Remind yourself about your body.
- Do yourself a favor and go with your partner to a vernissage or concert. Take yourself and your thoughts away from the routine of everyday life.
- Take yourself on a date! Sit down in a nice cafe, order your favorite coffee or cocktail. Observe others, smile at them.

Remember that humans are a pack animal, we can transfer amazing energy to ourselves, and meeting people is often an interesting experience. You don't believe me? Try to remind yourself about it.

- Put your phone and computer in one drawer. Forget, at least for an hour, about the ubiquitous technology that often overloads us with unnecessary information.

The relaxation time you spend recharging your batteries will work like a rejuvenating injection. It will allow you to forget about mental and physical fatigue – it's up to you for how long. If you introduce the battery charging ritual into your life, you will notice its measurable benefits after a short time. From improved well-being, better concentration and memory, through efficiency and readiness to act. Everything in nature requires balance, remember that you are one of its integral parts.

FROM THE AUTHOR'S NOTEBOOK

The snow was still falling – April 2010

The snow was still falling, freezing air of –15 degrees moved the trees and made them freeze, the days remained dark and sad.

The cold paralyzed my feelings, emotions, joy. Paralyzed my heart.

And it was snowing again, and now an icy rain was coming. I covered myself with layers of clothes to keep my muscles from going numb, let alone my heart.

It went on for days, weeks, months. Many, many hours in the dark.

Many, many hours alone.

Winter seemed endless it seemed the sun would never rise. I'm tired of waiting, I'm tired of hoping!

Pretending a smile, I didn't feel like, turning on the light in the morning, going out into the street, what for? To meet this cursed cold? I didn't feel the need to find people, friends, call them, invite them home. And ask them to keep each other company. I lost it. Everything has lost its meaning.

I stopped caring about my appearance, bathing, giving up hope. I lost her. I chose darkness, apathy and solitude.

Being locked up at home in pajamas all day gave me some security. For what would I want to see more people? What could I talk to them about? I didn't have much to say.

Weeks passed, colder and quieter. Loneliness engulfed me. I've run out of words, I missed music.

My body conceived to react with nausea, numbness, weakness.

It started with headaches, and then stomach pains, now breathing problems, my eyesight began to fail me, being much more tired. Now the mood and the head again.

I just let myself be destroyed, I gave up, I had no more strength, I lost myself, there was no part of me that would whisper **"you are alive, so live"**. *I no longer had the urge to be angry or fight for whatever purpose. More hours of sleep. Winter continued and my heart froze too, it was covered like grass with so many layers of snow and cold. It didn't move anywhere, didn't know how to cry or how to feel.*

It was neither happy nor bad. I stopped being interested in everything. And at the same time everything annoys me.

I heard 2 unique voices in the distance, but I didn't feel myself in the same melody as them, what could I offer them when I didn't even have anything for myself? Why do they rejoice? How do they do it? Stupid household duties sometimes forced me to get out of bed, but my condition, and this strength that made me unable to move from here and all this physical and mental pain prevented me from doing so. Slight tachycardia began, terror and at the same time an internal desire for an immediate, deadly disease. Worrying, going back to the hospital, analyses, doctors' opinions, stress. A lot of stress and thinking maybe it's over.

My body and mind screamed **"Please help me. Please look at me, I'm here"** ... **"do not leave me."**

I finally understood the signals my body was sending me. I started to soften. I realized that I want what I have and what I care about.

People, who surround me, are for me extremely important and yes, I need them.

Yes, I love myself and I want the sun to rise again in my life. I want to turn on music and fill my home, my family with joy. Nothing stands in the way of moving, eating and laughing.

My body began to disintegrate, remnants from months of neglect were everywhere. Diarrhea, vomiting, runny nose that was still present, dandruff. Finally... tears. Tears that heal.

For the last two days I feel much better, I took a shower with great desire. I don't get tired anymore I have no difficulty breathing whenever I leave the house.

Today I am able to talk about all this. When I was inside the spider's web, I couldn't find words to express what I felt. Now I can confidently ask for hugs like when I was a child, that I never really stopped being.

I put on some make-up, put on clothes that still fit me well, put on my favorite perfume...

I put enough blush on my cheeks to cover the yellowish skin that looks like it never saw the sun. Lots of concealer for dark circles under the eyes, lots of mascara. I fixed my hair, it was silky, shiny and strong... big surprise of the day... I looked beautiful... I was the most wonderful pregnant woman that ever walked the earth!

I left the bedroom. There was so much light outside... Suddenly I heard the sound of laughter. When I entered the room, four eyes greeted me as if I had never left the room.

I saw two smiles. I finally felt in my place. It has begun my recovery.

The price for not going home to Mexico in the early months of my pregnancy, when I had the opportunity, was too high. The harsh, long and dark winter added to the delicate state I was in. All of this worked against me.

I won't do it again. Next time I'll think about my own limits. Even if everyone thinks I am selfish and reckless, I will think of myself.

I don't want to try survive. I want to live.

I am not a pine tree. I can't be a pine tree. I am a sunflower.

EMOTIONAL INTELLIGENCE

Emotional intelligence is the ability to understand, use and manage one's emotions in order to relieve stress, communicate effectively and empathize with others, overcome challenges and defuse conflicts.

Emotional intelligence is one of the most important qualities that is worth developing in yourself on an ongoing basis. Contacting with other people – partners, children, friends from work or neighbors, makes us establish relationships that become valuable for both parties over time.

Daniel Goleman*, an American psychologist in his book *"Emotional Intelligence"*, showed how important it is in life on the way to success and happiness. The researcher points out that the number of emotional problems around the world is increasing day by day. Depression, which is diagnosed in an increasing number of the population and is more and more often mentioned in media. As a society, we are getting richer, but we pay the highest price – our own happiness.

Developing emotional intelligence will give us the tools to manage our lives, resist attacks from some people and behave appropriately towards others in harmony with ourselves. This balance will ultimately translate into an emotional life, thanks to which we will start to build a strong emotional bond with loved ones and that results in opening up to the fullness of love.

There are several factors that characterize emotional intelligence:

Self-awareness is knowing yourself

It is the ability to recognize the emotions that overwhelm us. As a consequence, we understand ourselves better, we develop self-esteem. Greater control and awareness of emotions let us control our lives and make better decisions.

---

* **Daniel Goleman** (born March 7, 1946) is an author, psychologist, and science journalist. Has written books on topics including self-deception, creativity, transparency, meditation, social and emotional learning, eco literacy and the ecological crisis.

Self-regulation, i.e., the ability to manage emotions

Controlling emotions is one of the most important issues that builds our self-control. It is extremely important in the learning process to regulate them so that they do not take over our lives. It is also the ability to quickly get out of emotional problems. Then we develop the ability to calm down, free ourselves from sadness or anger. Often their self-control leads to a quick recovery, helps to rise faster after a failure.

Motivation, which is the art of subordinating emotions to specific goals

All our drives and mechanisms – biological, social and psychological, do not allow us to remain idle, pushing us constantly to action. Motivation determines the goals we strive for, while emotions reflect the state of feelings we experience while trying to achieve these goals.

Empathy is a gift that distinguishes us from other animals, giving us the ability to empathize with the emotions of other beings

Awareness of feelings, needs or understanding of other people, sensitivity to their feelings, has a measurable impact on our social contacts. Recognizing the sensitive tissue in a person translates into helping and taking the perspective from the other person's point of view, which has a very positive impact on interpersonal relationships. Empathic people are more sensitive to the social signals sent by others, which allows them to react appropriately to them.

Social skills that make it easy for us to establish and maintain contact with other people

Establishing and maintaining contacts refers to the ability to show a range of emotions in a relationship, the most important thing is that they have a positive dimension, thanks to which we infect each other with what is good.

Example: Kate and Anthony are going on a paradise holiday to Belize. When they arrive, the man confesses his love to Kate, proposing to her in a beautiful scenery. Kate feels that she is the luckiest girl in the world. However, on the fifth day of their stay, Anthony gets drunk and confesses to her that during their relationship, he cheated on her on a business trip. Kate breaks into a million of pieces, unable to forgive her beloved. She breaks off the engagement and moves out of their house. She will spend the next few years rejecting Anthony's pleas for forgiveness, she will heal her broken heart, hating every member of the male species, and she will carry this pain and grief all her life.

Upon learning about Anthony's confession, Kate has the right to feel strong emotions. However, it is a mistake to remove a loved one from your life. If she had been emotionally intelligent, she would have waited out the first and second storm of emotions around them. After returning home, analyzing Anthony's advantages and disadvantages, she decides that she loves him and does not want to live without him. After the first series of screams and tears resulting from

41

the pain of feeling betrayed, she would give the man one more chance, believing that they were made for each other.

Emotional intelligence is not to be confused with empathy and making excuses for not being in control of your emotions. When someone inflicts pain on us, it is important to get rid of it – both by screaming and confronting the one who caused us this pain.

Emotional intelligence, however, allows you to manage your feelings and adjust them to the situation. Psychologists mostly agree that it is not passed down genetically, it can be learned through clearly defined rules.

An emotionally intelligent person is open to the world and people, manages emotions depending on the situation in which they participate, does not allow oneself to be manipulated, but also does not manipulate others. Most often, such people easily cope with stress without transferring it onto others. They understand criticism and are not afraid to take risks, thanks to which they benefit in many fields – professionally and privately.

We build emotionally intelligent relationships every day at home among our family members and friends. We translate this experience every time we interact with other people. If we are able to identify reality, look at it from many perspectives, analyze it correctly with proper emotional management, then we solve conflicts faster, we do not get bogged down in problematic situations. As a consequence, freeing ourselves from what is destructive and negative for us, we live in greater harmony with people and the environment. With this in mind, we will be more successful in our social relationships.

**Improve yourself for your partner,
but most of all for yourself.**

Improving ourselves should be the primary goal of each of us. Our attitude is the most important factor on the way to change for the better. From today on, try not to associate self-improvement with work, followed by discouragement and fatigue. The desires to be a better person, more aware of one's needs and desires, should strengthen and motivate us on the way to fulfilling them. Try to learn from your mistakes. Let all the metaphorical pebbles that fall into your shoe become a challenge for you, which you will overcome with a smile on your face. Don't give up, stop succumbing to bad luck, it's like the wheel of fortune.

**Your good attitude is the key
to breaking the deadlock.**

Learn to draw strength from your inconveniences. None of us today can count on getting special treatment. We live in a world of perfectly-imperfect people.

The only thing that remains constant in life is change.

If you neglected, forgot or simply did not have time, remind yourself how important the psychospiritual sphere is in human development. What fuel it is for us, which recharges us every morning, activates us to take on new challenges. Suddenly, every day becomes more fruitful and satisfying.

You are the creators of your own life!

Exercise

It is often worth confronting your own taste, character and check-ing the differences that have occurred over the years. Is Brad Pitt still your ideal of masculinity and Angelina Jolie of femininity? As your favorite dish you will choose as your No. 1 – pork chop with potatoes, or maybe today it is pasta with spinach? Such tests allow us to return to ourselves and our long-made choices. Redefining them.

See how much they have changed?

Ask yourself some questions

- What do I like to do most in my free time with my partner?
- What makes me truly happy?
- What is my relationship with my partner's family?
- Which family member is closest to me and why?
- Do I feel professionally fulfilled?
- Three people I admire are…
- My favorite body parts are…
- What character traits do I envy my partner?

If you had a problem with this task, it's time to work on it. Allow yourself to become your best friend and you will see how fate and other people – both friends and strangers – will start to treat you. Sounds like magic?

Experience it.

Look your best, feel as good as possible!

From both, general knowledge and sociological research, it is clear that our appearance is of great importance. Even if we wanted it to be different, denied it, discussed the advantages of interior values over exterior looks, it is not the other way around, and probably – it will never be. Our appearance largely affects how we feel and how we are perceived.

People who feel good in their own skin do better in social life. Our appearance translates into general functioning as a partner relationship, in work and amongst friends.

We perceive well-groomed people as resourceful, full of strength and abilities, we forgive those more and are more willing to help them, and we make friends with them faster.

It is obvious that we do not have influence on every aspect of our appearance, some things cannot be changed and the faster we accept it, the better for us. However, let's never forget about taking care of ourselves, let's try to be the best version of ourselves every day.

**Thanks to a well-groomed appearance,
life is easier for us.**

Exercise

Remember this morning, you looked at your reflection in the mirror and what feelings did you have? Did you like what you saw? With what attitude did you leave home and enter your workplace?

Remember that people initially judge us primarily by appearance. However, real long-lasting relationships are established not because of your looks, but because of character and knowledge, which is why it is so important to work on yourself.

This is probably the best time to make changes that will bring you success. We often forget that life is a constant series of changes. The only thing that doesn't change about it is the fact of changes that we experience.

Believe that you can make yourself feel better in an easy and pleasant way. Take some time to bring out your inner beauty. The effects will not be visible immediately. Consistent work on yourself, establishing daily beauty rituals, will make your self-confidence skyrocket, making it easier for you to make contact with both men and women.

Exercise

Try to sit in silence and even out your breath. Do you feel calm? Start a conversation with yourself, listen to yourself. Ask questions and answer them, be good and honest with yourself:

- With what attitude did you get out of bed today?
- What are your strong character traits?
- What distinguishes you from others?
- Which personality traits get you into trouble?
- What dreams do you have?
- What are you feeling now?
- How will you start your day tomorrow?

These simple questions become extremely difficult when we have to be honest with ourselves. Most often, the answers are surprising to us, knocking us out of the sense in which we have lived so far.

Your joy and satisfaction will make everyday duties easier; the world will be more open and people will be friendly.

How often and to what extent do you take care of your mental hygiene compared to:

- Keeping the body in physical balance, dedicating a specific amount of time to movement or sport.
- Taking care of your appearance, including: clothes styling, hairdo, make-up or keeping mustaches and beards in good shape.
- Routine medical examination.
- Performing tests, which you then verify with specialists.
- Supplementing the body according to guidelines.

There is nothing more valuable for the overall psychophysical condition than proper care of mental hygiene. Allowing the free flow of thoughts and emotions without fixating on the negative aspects that are inseparable from our existence will make us feel better.

Is there anything more valuable than living with positive good energy every day?!

Are you aware of how many negative experiences, situations and thoughts generated every day have a negative impact on your well-being, and ultimately on the actions you take?

Realize that you can't get rid of some "*mental garbage*"; they are a natural consequence of interpersonal relationships and the routine of everyday life. However, being aware of this, work on ensuring that they do not become the sole food for your psyche and intellect. The destructive consequences of this process could degrade you in your own eyes.

Exercise

Think about your psyche:

- Do you maintain mental hygiene, free flow of thoughts, work on well-being?
- How often do you deliver something good for your mind?
- How often do you throw *"mental garbage"* out of your head?

Imagine being able to make a mental selection of everything that reaches your psyche and be aware to separate what is profitable and useful for you and discard what does not serve you.

Example: Zoe is preparing spaghetti bolognese for dinner with Rafael. At the stage of straining the pasta, she pours out the cloudy water that is no longer needed. Think of this cooking process as an analogy to our lives.

Cloudy water symbolizes thoughts and unnecessary emotions that we absorb every day, and the pasta itself is the content that we should feed on, i.e., our pleasant experiences.

Remember to take time at least three times a week to analyze what is worth separating from yourself and what is useful for you to absorb.

Erase from your memory all the toxic and hurtful words and actions that have been "*fed*" to you in the past. Nowadays you are a different person, love this person and do not allow other people and personal exhausting emotions to affect the quality of your life.

Our head is like an ocean, and our thoughts are like waves – they come and go. Statistically, a person has between 60,000 and 80,000 thoughts a day. They accompany us all day, helping us to assess reality, evaluate it and find answers to it. Conscious control over them is extremely important. Stress, overstimulation, negative content has an aggravating effect on us, exhausting the body physically and mentally. Often in such situations, being out of tune, we can lose important things that are currently happening in our lives and those of our loved ones off the radar.

Another issue is trying to stop thoughts that affect our development destructively. The best way to imagine this is when we put a dam on a flood wave, without trying to deal with its accumulation. Sooner or later this practice will cause the dam to be broken, flooding us with consequences. In extreme cases, drowning us.

Thoughts, whether we like it or not, will keep coming from all directions. Sometimes your mind will seem like a calm sea, other times there will be thunder storms. However, thoughts accompany us all day, without our will, helping us to assess reality, evaluate it and find answers. Learning to digest and select which thoughts to give importance to and which to allow to float away is extremely important. Practicing meditation is an excellent way to train the mind to discern thoughts. Otherwise, it is easy to fall into stress, overstimulation and negative content, which has an aggravating effect on us, exhausting the body physically and mentally. Often in such situations, being out of tune, we can miss important things that are currently happening in our lives and those of our loved ones off the radar.

GET OUT OF YOUR COMFORT ZONE

The comfort zone is a safe place to which we are used to, where we do not feel threatened by anything, but also not stimulated by anything new.

It is natural to fall into habits, patterns, actions on so-called autopilot.

Every time you leave your comfort zone, you experience extreme emotions – curiosity, excitement, but also fear and discomfort. The reaction of our body depends on the intellectual and emotional backbone. If you are open, you accept **new opportunities that life gives you, you have the chance to discover and have more.**

Stagnation has a destructive effect on people and relationships between them. Remember to show the world and specially yourself the best of you. Be open to different possibilities, take healthy risks, and meet new people. Challenge yourself every day and most importantly – overcome your fears!

Turn off stress

Life is here and now. When you practice being in the present as a priority, you notice and understand more. Your quality of life will dramatically improve. Find at least 20 minutes a day to spend for yourself.

Probably many of you, accustomed to having the day full of activities, reading about finding twenty minutes of free time during the day, make a grimace on your face. It is important that you try.

Keep in the back of your mind that it's worth working on yourself in moments when you don't devote one hundred percent of your concentration and attention to something. Such moments are a norm for us on a daily basis.

From walking the dog, brushing teeth, cooking, vacuuming, or even when you're waiting for the green light. Let every seemingly trivial act be enriched by your self-reflection. Time spent with yourself is of great value!

These are the moments that calm us down, allow us to better understand our life. If you feel that you don't like spending time with yourself, you feel uncomfortable in moments of silence, when you don't have something to do and you feel the urge to reach to looking at your phone constantly, it's time to make a change and start reversing this process. Start working on reversing this process. We tend to talk badly about ourselves, we internalize the words and feelings of others towards us, which is often destructive to our physical and mental health.

Go for a walk, explore your surroundings or explore new paths. Try to pay attention to the sounds, sights, smells and textures you encounter. Immerse yourself in nature that will strengthen you and calm you down. Come home, take a warm, relaxing bath or shower. If you don't have the time for that due to family obligations, wait until the household is asleep.

Follow your intuition and impulses

Adults often ignore the fact that the youngest are one of the most reliable sources of information – they honestly and without hesitation tell what the world around them is like. Thanks to their great imagination, they become a source of inspiration and fun. Make the most of their colorful world and imitate their perception! The youngest follow their innate sense of intuition and impulses. To attract love, find and then follow your inner child.

Make creative goals

To improve your attitude towards the world, it is worth making new, creative goals for yourself. It can be either a new passion, sport, volunteering for a charity organization or returning to learning a foreign language. Once you start, be consistent. Follow your plan and learn new things.

Connection is essential

After achieving the goal, it is worth reaching out to people and informing them about your experiences. Connect with others regularly and try to listen to what inspires others. Depending on your willingness, you can engage in a new community to experience acceptance and a sense of belonging in a new environment. Changing or expanding the group of friends is always an interesting experiment, it opens the horizons of thought, bringing us closer to other people.

Take some time to make peace with your body and allow it to feel. Find out what it likes. Watch it, admire it. Start, for example, by savoring the food you put in your mouth. Leave your cell phone while you eat and experience the different flavors that pass through your palate. Pay attention to your senses. Lose yourself in them. In addition to the fact that this practice lands you in the here and now, the activation of your senses can be very enriching for your self-awareness and development. Remember that when you allow yourself to savor and experience pleasure using your senses, your body rewards you by releasing hormones directly related to the feeling of happiness.

FROM THE AUTHOR'S NOTEBOOK

Eyes open meditation – July 2018

At times like these, when my mind, body, and soul come together, I almost feel like I'm floating, as if I'm levitating. Then I have close contact with nature. I am relaxed.

With the presence of God by my side, or maybe in God, or God in my being. I would like to be able to convey this beauty that I feel now, this peace, this love, completeness and harmony in my mind.

I will try to describe it.

Thoughts and ideas continue to flutter everywhere. No direction. It is a state similar to meditation, but with eyes open, sharpened senses and a naked soul. I feel heat around me, but it doesn't bother me. I hear music, voices, birds.

Each sound appears separately, and at the same time intertwines and complements one another. They don't bother each other they do not overshadow each other.

They just learned to respect, tolerate and let each other exist.

But my mind doesn't fight them, it doesn't connect to anything, it doesn't stop, it doesn't prevent them by trying to squeeze or torture them. It neither judges them like a judge in a court nor persecutes them. Does not glorify them or put pressure on them and ask them to say more. It just allows them to exist. To be.

And then the clouds and the trees, the bee and the mountains, being so far apart, become one. And then my being appears in this picture and becomes a mountain, a bee, a cloud.

So naturally.

It is so obvious that we are one. It seems funny to me that I didn't realize it before.

There is silence, and at the same time I hear everything with such precision, with such attention, with an intense force that stuns.

But there is also silence.

Not just mine, it belongs to whoever that wants it. To anyone who wants to appreciate it. Everything around me is created, so that I can contemplate and enjoy myself.

It's painted for me and it is mine for now.

There it is.

There it was, waiting for the owner. Many or none.

And so, it had to happen for me to be here at this moment, today, in this place and give up myself to become a part of everything. I stop to bother and care, or I stop notice that I left my glasses in the case, in the bag, at home, and my lazy left eye sees only what it wants to see.

I stop seeing with my eyes, I see with my soul.

And I breathe.

I feel my lungs fill with air and I am now part of the grass. Part of the notes.

I realize that I have been in the same position for a while without paying attention. I suddenly feel uncomfortable.

Really it is very uncomfortably. Finally, I have changed my position.

I got so far that for a few seconds (or minutes, maybe it took forever?) I stopped thinking about myself.

I didn't want anything… I didn't need anything.

I felt no thirst or heat, and have not felt discomfort.

It was as if the air I was breathing and the air moving the clouds were the same.

The buzzing of a fly has been integrated with the music. In harmony.

I'm back.

Different voices, big and small, remind me it's time to go back and they need something.

They want something, at least my attention.

Feet were on the ground again. But however,…

However … this memory, this state of unity, separation and wholeness, I will keep with me.

I will take this with me.

And at the same time, I stayed here.

"ROAD TO THE DESTINATION"

The goals we set and achieve throughout our lives prevent us from acting like a lost child in a fog. Cause and effect are written in the narrative of life, which is why it is so important to get to know yourself and your needs, and then implement them in your life. It is crucial that the road to a goal is like a journey to your desired destination. Each of them is divided into individual stages. Try to have in mind the feeling of satisfaction that comes over you when you do it.

Remember that the very process of reaching a goal is already a great achievement! Don't just reward yourself only at the finish line. May the effort of your work be rewarded more often.

Read this sentence again, close your eyes and imagine it – isn't this method easier to face challenges?

Your psychic revolution will not happen immediately. Every process takes time. The more sophisticated and complicated it is, the longer it takes to reach the finish line, but how much more satisfying!

Learn that hard work in the field of healing your emotions. Getting out of difficulties, fears and reaching stabilization of the mental sphere is the most profitable investment in a happy life.

It is important not to make unnecessary self-criticism and not to give up when something does not work out right away. Mistakes and mishaps are inherent in every project of our lives. Without them, a person does not learn, does not develop properly. If everything in life was as easy as getting from our bed to the bathroom, our existence would be flat and boring.

Example: Maria decided to accomplish one of her biggest dreams – to learn to play the piano. However, she did not think that the development of a new passion is associated with work that required such focus and time. Learning the notes, getting to know the instrument are tedious stages. At first, her fingers and hands ached, but after the first week, when she played John a small fragment of his favorite piece composed by Chopin, it turned out to be a breakthrough moment in her development – not only in the context of learning to play the piano.

Every effort sooner or later will be noticed and rewarded, it's only a matter of time.

THE SMART PRINCIPLE

The SMART principle, which we borrow from the language of business, is an acronym – it is the combination of the first letters of words that you should familiarize yourself with and note them as effective tools that you will rely on during your journey to a goal, thanks to which your chances of achieving it will increase.

Specific

- What do you actually care about?
- What will achieving your goal bring you?

Measurable

- What will change after reaching the goal?
- How will you benefit from this fact?

Attainable

- What is the reason for achieving this goal?
- Are your reasons strong enough to embark on a long-term goal?

Relevant

- Example: Is moving with the whole family to Australia in the next few months realistic or rather in the sphere of dreams? Maybe it's enough to change the location to the seaside.
- Will it really pay off for you?

Time-related

- Is one year enough to achieve your goal? Or does it take 2 years? Pour the proverbial bucket of cold water over yourself, and then write down in your calendar the actual time you have to work towards achieving it.

- Is your strategy the most appropriate? Maybe it's worth rethinking the whole thing.

The current times are extremely demanding, we are bombarded with information that is not necessarily useful to us. Overstimulation makes us apathetic or vice versa – nervous and hyperactive. The fact that in addition to your professional work you have some ambitions, plans and dreams already should make you proud of yourself!

Success is just around the corner, just give yourself a little time to meet it.

Have in mind that a seed planted in the ground takes time to come to the surface. Many of us get discouraged shortly before the stem breaks out of the ground.

BEING RESPONSIBLE
FOR YOUR WORDS AND ACTIONS

This is a trait that is currently in the phase of disappearance in modern society, but it makes life easier for us and others. I am talking about being responsible for yourself. One of the most common mistakes that I see in my practice is to blame others for what is happening to you. To live your own life felling like you are the victim of your history and evading responsibility for your own actions. For example, it is wrong to think that a therapist will do everything for us.

A professional psychotherapist helps you develop the right tools and is like a blank canvas on which you paint the effects of working with and on yourself. Guided individually, you observe the successive progress of changes that ultimately contribute to painting a new picture – one of yourself.

When you feel that you are ready to take complete responsibility for yourself and every aspect of your life, then you are freeing yourself from the sense of grievance that often weighs us down. You are not alone in feeling that the relationships you have entered into have most often ended in failures or semi-failures at best. Unfortunately, the coronavirus pandemic has deepened the social mood, in which we increasingly feel let down by the people around us. It's worth learning to live with it. Learn lessons from negative experiences. Try to break out from blaming people for the evil and its manifestations that have happened to you on the line of life. Pessimistic thinking will not help you or your present and future relationships in building their strong foundation, without which it is difficult to think of a stable structure.

Why is taking the consequences of your actions so important for self-healing?

Life is the energy of action so we naturally also affect the existence of others. With this in mind and taking responsibility for what we have done, are doing and will do, the repercussions of actions will affect us with less and less force. We live in social patterns.

Most actions and behaviors are repeated, so we have a chance not to make the same mistake twice. When you understand that your every action cause reaction – which is inevitable in the process of life – the sooner you will have the need to control yourself. Self-control affects every aspect of our lives. It leaves a visible mark on our image.

Believe me, this fact will be quickly noticed and, most importantly, appreciated by your environment.

WHEN WE LOVE TOO MUCH

"*Loving too much*" is a problem for many people, most of whom are women, according to research. The well-known American psychotherapist Robin Norwood has written many insightful works on this subject. According to her, "*loving too much*" is staying in a relationship that isn't satisfying. Such a relationship causes pain and suffering, triggering a feeling of rejection or humiliation in us. However, despite this – or maybe because of this – we decide to stay in a complicated, often destructive relationship.

Loving too much ultimately involves a destructive force where you are most often in a bad mood, you lack strength and motivation, you suffer both mentally and physically.

You have no motivation for anything, you persistently think about the object of your affection, sometimes bringing yourself to the very bottom. It is often difficult to cut ties alone and put your life back together. Such a life situation requires the intervention of caring relatives or a professional therapist.

What makes us love too much?

Most often, as in many other dysfunctions that manifest themselves in relationships, it is influenced by a number of childhood experiences.

These were houses with strict rules, distance in the relationships with parents or siblings, lack of proper patterns of love, which makes us handicapped in building our own home.

Growing up in a dysfunctional environment, where emotional needs were not met, often accompanied by loneliness and fear, they create our worldview and interactions with it, causing that when approaching another person, we pour over a large stream of feelings, that were previously suppressed.

Many scientists, psychologists and addiction therapists compare *"loving too much"* to the feeling of being addicted to drugs or alcohol. We become addicted to being with the other person, doing everything to spend as much time with them as possible. When they are missing in our environment, we do not stop thinking about them, longing and becoming more and more obsessed.

Such a strong feeling becomes a strategy that we build most often in our subconscious.

Its goal is to overcome old experiences, deal with the past, and fight the feeling that the partner will reject us for the slightest mistake, temporary weakness, and trifle.

**What signals and behaviors can mean
that we *"love too much"*?
Here are some features you should pay attention to:**

Sacrifice

Staying in a relationship despite feeling hurt, not feeling happy and secure. Women often assume the role of *"mothers"* in such relationships, and men of *"fathers"*. Sometimes such people assume the role of friends or even therapists. Often people who *"sacrifice"* look for the basis of their unhappiness in their partners. They see solutions to problems in them, assuming that if the partners are happy, they will be too.

Feeling guilty

People who "*love too much*" often live in guilt, shame and fear of not being good enough, tender or attractive enough. This leads to blaming yourself for any bad moods, failures or even mental and physical violence against them at the hands of a partner.

Obsession, control and fear of rejection

A person who has become "*obsessed*" with the relationship focuses solely on the needs and problems of the partner. Unfortunately, the problem is often exacerbated by the submissiveness of the person who loves more. The partner who dominates the relationship begins to take advantage of her morbid subordination and the fact that she is able to forgive practically everything. Obsessive attachment to a partner pushes feelings of anger, pain, and injustice further into the subconscious. However, as is the habit of the human psyche, all demons are carefully hidden – sooner or later they will reveal themselves.

Fear of intimacy

People who "*love too much*" often do not experience a feeling of security in the early years of their lives, it is difficult for them to enter into a relationship. Close contact with a partner destroys their worldview. They often equate intimacy with rejection, any relationship based on devotion and trust destroys their self-knowledge standards.

Fear of loneliness

All those who love too much have in common the fact that after entering into a relationship, discovering the values of being in a relationship, they are ultimately terrified of losing the new path they have entered. Returning to loneliness, not sharing life with someone, fighting the feeling of loneliness again paralyzes them. When they think that they are about to return to feeling insecure again, they make them defend this relationship using all possible methods known. Self-justification and rationalization of actions taken to keep a partner with you are often associated with making irrational decisions, mood swings, and even aggression toward others or self-harm. In the most complicated cases, to suicide attempts.

Getting lost

People affected by the lack of intimacy with a parent may live with a feeling of unsatisfied love, which leads to the feeling of losing themselves in love for their partner. We often deal with a distorted image of a partner, idealizing their image both in the mind and in the heart. In addition, they feel a lack of affection from their partner all the time, constantly having to verify it and check it in various ways. Without being aware of it, people who love too much perceive the relationship as if it were a distorted mirror of imaginary standards and needs.

Great euphoria of being with a partner

We know that being with a partner gives us great joy. However, if this causes us to lose quality in dealing with anyone else, then a red light should light up for us. The relationship with a partner should not have a negative impact on our relationships with other people.

The desire to have the other person exclusively

In not so extreme cases, it can bear the hallmarks of morbid jealousy. When we are jealous of other people of the opposite sex around our partner, it still seems quite normal, but when this jealousy extends to your partners' loved ones – parents, children, siblings – it is disturbing.

Pressure on your partner to extend your time together

Words like *"don't go yet"* or *"don't go out with them, I want to spend the weekend together"* often show a strong interest in a partner. However, every relationship should have clearly defined boundaries. They often expand when they are in the process of falling in love. Later, we accuse ourselves of neglecting our loved ones like family and friends, sometimes losing some of them even forever.

Loss of identity in order to please a partner

Most of us have interests and passions, whether it's fitness, skiing, dancing or crocheting. If we give up following our passions just because our partner does not share them, it is a sign that we are neglecting ourselves, sacrificing an integral part of our personality for the sake of a relationship. Let's keep in mind, that by losing our identity piece by piece, which, after all, was an element of what attracted our partner to us, we condemn ourselves to changes in ourselves.

Personality disorder

This is one of the more delicate issues in human life, because changing our reactions is difficult to observe, thanks to the fact that each of us is different. This is why self-observation is so important.

We talk about personality disorders when our attitude towards the world changes to negative, we withdraw from social life, we show an excessive willingness to direct and manipulate others.

Change of life plans

It is natural that our vision of life changes when we enter a new relationship. If we had polarized life and professional plans, let's not lose them completely on account of the relationship – at least not during the so-called honeymoon period. A good relationship is one in which each party feels fulfilled in life and ambition.

Loss of decision-making ability

In a successful relationship, decisions are made together. We want to count on our partner or we look for confirmation of our actions and plans in them. However, let's leave some spheres of life only to ourselves. Let's not let a particularly dominant partner influence every change.

If you feel that the problem may concern you, it is extremely important to start rebuilding your self-esteem, independence and autonomy. Learning to return to being independent, extending the period of being away from the presence of a partner is extremely important in creating ourselves.

There is nothing worse than cornering, controlling your partner and vice versa.

The signaling reactions are the feeling of mental and physical pain as soon as the partner is no longer with us. Such an example is the routine departure of the partner to work, while the other person is waiting for him all the time in a feeling of longing and hope that the time of his return home will come soon.

BEING TOGETHER,
BUT SEPARATELY

Each of us has a need to be independent. After the "*honeymoon*" phase, during which we spent time almost exclusively with the other half – after all, for balance – we return to the bosom of friends and family.

We all need to be alone with ourselves, but we also feel the need to meet new people while being in a relationship. The first dangers in this natural process of reintegration into society appear when your partner or you – keep pushing, complaining, asking, or manipulating facts – wanting at all costs to spend the same amount of time with the other half as at the beginning of the relationship. Such methods can quickly lead to cornering and eventually your partner will distance themselves from you instead of approaching you.

The unequal struggle of needs and desires between the partners becomes disturbed, reluctance appears, which ultimately resembles a vicious circle.

If our partner wants to go out to others, they have such a need, all attempts to keep them at home, express disapproval, will make them think about having more freedom, which, taking into account the dark scenario, will be the first step towards conflicts in the relationship.

After emotional stabilization, each side should return to the developed scenarios for their own lives – this will improve the energy and hygiene in the relationship.

In my practice, I have come across a case where one of the parties was not ready to loosen the bond. However, she decided to remain silent while her partner went out to friends and returned to his passions. At that time, his partner felt mental pain so strong that her emotional state translated into physical health, and somatic symptoms led her to serious illness and hospitalization.

Example: Andrew needs to go out with his friends three times a week while Hanna prefers to spend this time together. The couple sits down together, talks about their needs. Then Andrew limits going out with friends to two times a week, but Hanna internally does not agree to it, she suffers when her partner is not around. The woman's mental pain causes her to experience numerous inflammations in her body, which eventually end up in surgery. Andrew, seeing the serious condition of his partner, is present with her throughout the hospitalization period. Hanna sees how the illness has affected her partner's behavior and brought them back together. The woman begins to use this against them.

Numerous manipulations and the fact of reluctance to recover from the disease, most often subconsciously, may end up driving the partners away from each other. When Andrew notices that his partner's illness is prolonged indefinitely, and he is not allowed to meet his needs, frustration sooner or later will outweigh the scales of bonding with his other half.

At this stage, intervention and honest conversation are necessary, analyzing where you are in the relationship and how much you are able to sacrifice for it.

Find time and space for an honest conversation, but if you feel that the topic is too difficult or your emotions are too complicated, use the help of an experienced couple's therapist.

In the event that we miss our own needs and plans for the future, our pace of commitment to the relationship is dangerously different. Let your partner get to your point, don't rush him, let go of further progress. Often less is more and this rule is worth sticking to in this case.

Example: Andrew loves Hanna, he wants to be in a relationship with her, but it is also important for him to regain his old life. He makes numerous attempts to invite her to go out together with friends, but she definitely refuses, preferring to stay home alone, consciously or not – then she puts herself in the role of a victim, deepening her pain and frustration. Such denial of the problem or vice versa – deepening it – can lead to serious disagreements between the partners.

In the opposite example, which I often encounter in my clinic. Caroline wants to return to her lifestyle before her relationship with Jerry. She loves to spend time at the gym, meet her friends there, take care of her perfect figure – it's time only for her. For the first time in her life, she feels that she has everything – a wonderful partner, a home to which she is happy to return. However, the fact that Jerry does not work out or practice any sports except for the winter ones, he works remotely from home, which means that their different lifestyles can lead to disputes and expectations that neither side is able to meet.

Exercise

Draw a line that you will mark at two points – at the beginning and at the end – on a scale of 1 to 10. Choose a point on the scale to what extent you need the attention and presence of your partner. For some it's 3 while for others it's 7–8 on the same scale.

    Think about where your partner's point on this scale is and what's the distance between you? If the distance is worryingly long, talk to each other honestly, at a time that is convenient for both of you. Try to figure out how to shorten this difference on the scale and what does it actually mean in your love life?

    Don't expect yourself to solve the problem with one conversation. Look for solutions from the inside, negotiate with each other, analyze the situation look for common solutions.

ENTERING A NEW RELATIONSHIP AND THE GHOSTS OF THE PAST

Many complications are brought to the relationship by a partner whose thinking is focused on finding the *"perfect half"* for himself. For example, years ago, he was in love with a girl he thought resembled the Hollywood beauty Scarlett Johanson. The relationship did not survive the test of time and character. Since then, the man has compared every woman he meets on the street to a Hollywood star.

An extremely important element in building a new relationship is the approach to the partner like a blank sheet of paper on which the fate of your relationship will be written.

Building a new house on old foundations often threatens its stability. At best, a life of fear, the consequences of which will be difficult to rebuild.

When the first differences of opinion creep into our lives, or vice versa, there is a ghostly silence, it is worth imagining that you are divided by a bridge, which is the only way to reconciliation, exit from conflict, and ultimately your way to happiness.

The rushing river that is under that represents the emotional burden, stress and situations resulting from living together, but also apart.

As I have mentioned before and will continue to use this argument to explain the many threats that currently lie in wait for romantic relationships – we live in extremely demanding times, where our psyche and spiritual sphere are constantly subjected to trials and challenges.

If there is a problem between you two and you feel that you are separated by a river, think about how much you are willing to sacrifice for this relationship on the way back to each other. It cannot be that one of the partners will always walk the whole way while the other half is standing or making a few insignificant movements. In the case of conflict resolution, good will is the overriding quality if we think about being together. A relationship is a job that both parties commit to with the same effort.

Example: John has always hated shopping for groceries, but Camila doesn't have time to constantly take care to having a full fridge. The couples agree that they will pick them up once a week from a well-stocked store, during the hours when traffic is the least.

Any conflict-producing situation can be solved with a good idea, which quickly turns out to be a sufficient solution to the conflict and the satisfaction of both parties.

Negative attitude and constantly fighting about small things have never brought measurable benefits to the relationship. Conflict is natural in a relationship. However, very often we forget about the power of hurtful words. Humiliating, challenging, recalling unpleasant issues from the past to build a stronger position in the conflict will ultimately only bring negative consequences. While one party feels victorious, the other is relegated to the role of the victim. Such solutions bring further disputes, the escalation of which is only a matter of time.

Both the dominant person, whose game can often be described as "*below the belt*", and the person in a losing, weaker position, if they do not find a solution to the conflict they are fighting in time, they will eventually come out of it badly injured. If you see or feel that a person close to you derives satisfaction from such situations or builds a strong life position thanks to such an attitude, do not negotiate, but break ties as soon as possible.

JEALOUSY

This is one of the most complicated and painful feelings that human nature has struggled with for centuries. Jealousy for the human psyche most often evokes a feeling of threat. It is most often accompanied by a range of destructive emotions, such as aggression, shame, fear or an overwhelming desire to control.

At the foundation of a relationship is the principle – without trust there is nothing. We often hear about couples who are insanely jealous of each other. Interestingly, some people find it romantic. Meanwhile, jealousy causes numerous limitations to the possibilities of personal development, which may contribute to the disorder of setting goals and their achievement. Similar to the construction of a house, work begins with solid foundations, not with the roof tiles.

The mechanism of jealousy can be compared to a loop that gradually tightens. It is characterized by a complicated emotional state. Numerous fears that we will lose what is most important to us – our loved one – can provoke the worst instincts in us.

We will defend what we love the most with all our strength and methods.

We must realize that jealousy is a typically human emotion that is natural not only to our species. However, releasing that in excess it can cause internal conflict and numerous external problems.

Often jealousy can be the first sign of your need to communicate with your partner about your needs, insecurities, boundaries and desires. It is very important that you sit down to such a conversation as soon as possible, which may seem difficult at first. However, its benefits can bring relief and a new beginning for your love.

Exercise

Take a piece of paper and write on it 5 examples of the last time you felt strong jealousy and where did it lead you? Think about how you expressed your jealousy. Analyze where jealousy comes from. Is it set for example in your partner, in the relationship that your partner has with another person? Do you have logical grounds for feeling jealous? Maybe you are comparing yourself to another person and think you are at a disadvantage? Would it help you work on raising your self-esteem?

If you feel that jealousy is one of the dominant emotions in your relationship, investigate what lies at the root of it. Start working on eliminating it from your life.

Where does your uncertainty come from?

Most jealousy stems from our insecurities. Often, by undermining the value we bring to a relationship, we are putting ourselves below the partner we want to spend our lives with. Remember that your partner wouldn't choose you if you weren't special. Remember that if someone decides to fall asleep with you and wake up with you every day, your presence has the greatest value for them.

Entering a new relationship, we bring a full package of experiences, not only those from the previous relationship, but also those that have accompanied us since childhood. If our previous partner was unfaithful and committed betrayals, and we have not worked through this trauma, we can be sure that to a greater or lesser extent, you will transfer this pain and uncertainty to the foundation of the new relationship.

It is worth approaching life both with an open mind and heart. There are currently over eight billion people on earth, among whom both we and our partner will find those who will seem attractive and interesting. Then it is worth setting a reasonable limit, where interest in the opposite sex is just drawing attention to someone, and when it turns into a cause for concern.

This point will come up often in this book, but it is the basis for the success of any relationship, whether love, friendship or work.

Communication is the foundation of any relationship!

When we are left alone, with a feeling of jealousy that is often one of the overwhelming and destructive ones. If we do not clarify the situation in advance, there is a risk that we will fall into a spiral of negative feelings, which sooner or later will end up in an explosion for us, which will lead to a fight.

It's worth talking. It is extremely important to cleanse ourselves of our anxieties, to confront the jealousy that begins to germinate in us. Are our fears real?

Let's try to take the perspective of another person, let's look at the problem with different eyes and different perspectives it will give us the opportunity to refresh our opinion, change our mood.

Do you ever get jealous of your partner's contact with a person of the opposite sex? Have you checked his/her phone, social media, looking over their shoulder?

This may mean that you are not controlling your jealousy by doing things that are ultimately an invasion of privacy for both parties. Beware of this, because the risk of being caught red-handed can lead to a drama that will be hard to get out of.

We often forget the power of simply writing down our feelings, concerns or reflections on a piece of paper. Writing is also one of the best ways to vent your emotions. Think back to how many people have healed themselves by writing diaries.

A diary was the first therapist for many people, including famous ones!

Remember that paper will accept everything, so it is worth using it. Separate positive thoughts from negative ones. Get into the habit of writing down all the bad scenarios on a piece of paper, and leaving the positive ones in your head.

After reading your negative thoughts, shred the peace of paper as if with you are leaving them in the past. This will not only help you heal your jealousy but clear your thoughts.

If you allow yourself to become comfortable in the multitude of dark thoughts, there is a risk that it will be very difficult for you to leave this state of affairs. Then you will expose your relationship to numerous risks.

Keeping jealousy in good shape will ultimately be destructive to our relationship, but also to relationships with other people. It is worth setting a rigid boundary when jealousy has grounds, and when our delusions, which are additionally fed, have a destructive effect on us.

PART II
"WE"

WHEN DO WE FEEL WE ARE IN A RELATIONSHIP?

In this chapter we will focus on the partnership relations which may turn out to be toxic or bear the hallmarks of such. How to deal with this? What to do to make your relationship have a chance to be and last for the best?

The expectations we have of a partner are much higher than those of friends, family, and co-workers. We enter a relationship with the belief that our other half will complement our shortcomings, often with all aspects of life in mind. In fact, the romantic term „*my other half*" implies that only with the presence of the partner, we will be complete. Which assumes that without it, we are not a whole.

As I mentioned before, it is very important to talk to your partner to deepen your bond. Every relationship that translates into a life together, right after the end of the so-called "*honeymoon*" phase, should start with common arrangements. But why didn't do this before? It would be much easier. Because in the honeymoon phase we usually don't pay attention at the differences between each other, or don't want to pay attention to them. We are too busy enjoying the hormones dance inside of us so, the decisions that we make are very often unconscious, dictated by passion and desire.

A relationship is a multifaceted connection, so we need to ask ourselves who we really are to each other and what benefits we get from this relationship. Of course, we are talking about emotions here, not about material values. This is the time when many couples who were not meant to be together break up. They were couples who were not looking for a serious and lasting relationship or the differences between them are so large that they (or one of them) decide not to stay together.

What is a lasting couple looking for? Emotional, mental, or physical support? The answer is simple, all these components.

The goals we set for ourselves in a healthy relationship should be based on our values, not material goals. I mention this because nowadays the problem of financing relationships is common and boils down to an exchange transaction in which it is difficult to look for a common future.

An obvious goal that can be qualified as material may be to build a house or start a business. However, we should prioritize personal goals. This includes the desire to start a family, to have and raise children, to stand up for other people, animals and the environment, to travel together. Belonging to religious groups, acting according to their ideas, participating in politics and so on.

These are important values that we talk about every day, and we make significant decisions about them. For the sake of the relationship, we should support each other.

In the case of building a common future, we must not forget about the fact that each of us is different and needs something different.

The relationship is not about unifying views, but respecting them by the other partner, listening to each other in an atmosphere of respect and understanding. Each of us, regardless of the social group to which we belong, has the right to their own beliefs, emotions, opinions, and choices.

Being and living among people on a daily basis is a great challenge. Most of us rush towards faster development,

society prefers material goods, ignoring the values of other people. Awareness of this fact has a chance to make people come back to themselves, as we used to do in the past.

We can confidently assume that in almost every relationship we require fidelity from each other. In addition to this issue, it is worth discussing other important topics before walking through the door marked *"serious relationship"*. I mean things related to home finances (not overspending or saving for a specific purpose), the issue of meeting friends and frequency of those meetings, alcohol consumption and so on.

THE IMPACT OF CONFLICT ON RELATIONSHIPS

Each partner has a different threshold of patience and a different limit at which they take part in a conflict. Even the first symptoms of tension in the relationship should make us stop and talk. It is important not to wait for the *"right moment"* **or transfer the problem to other aspects of life.** Much worse is waiting for a specific topic to appear and have you so irritated that you can no longer discuss or speak clearly, when patience and the desire to solve things instead of making them worse is gone.

Also, any kind of sweeping problems under the rug or denial can lead to irreversible changes. It is also worth realizing that there is no relationship without glitches, mistakes, conflicts, or difficult situations that seem to be the ones with no way out. Try to make friction enrich your relationship, learn from them lessons for the future. Try not to repeat the same mistakes.

Encode in your mind that it is worth every experience, even the worst, to enrich you with something, to make you realize something important. Each time you leave the comfort zone of your relationship, let it be a lesson for both parties.

Eliminate the phrases "*this destroyed me*", "*it ruins me*", "*we will never get through this*" from your vocabulary.

What areas of life are worth discussing and analyzing during the relationship?

Spiritual

Faith is a very important part of life for many people on earth. If people of different faiths enter a relationship, they must remember to respect their partner's beliefs and practices. In many cases, disputes arise against this background that is difficult to resolve.

Socio-social

When entering a new relationship, you must bear in mind that soon you will meet a group of people related to your partner, which includes family, friends and work colleagues. Some you will like others you will not, similarly with your other half who will enter your social circles. However, do not require your partner to break off contact with these people or avoid them. Likewise, the other way around. Such steps can have counterproductive results.

Political

Many countries are characterized by a multi-party democratic system, thanks to which everyone has the possibility to find an option close to their political and social values. However, if our other half has diametrically opposed views, frequent conflicts may arise on this background. Remember that the understanding and love unite you in this paramount.

Raising children

Each of us has taken certain values from home by which we try to live. In cases where they were disruptive or simply far from ideal – which made it difficult for you to function for years – we break with them to build a new system. Finding a consensus on how to raise your children is of great importance. Start building a plan for this important event in your life. Talk about what kind of parents you see in each other. And remember that there is no one good or right method of parenting.

Sexual sphere

As a rule, its strongest phase falls on the so-called *"honeymoon"* stage. At the time after getting to know each other, examining the partners, and sharing your own sexual needs, we show a similar degree of interest in sex. Over time, however, you may find that you have different levels and needs of satisfaction. Your preferences are flexible, so at some point you may find that they are different or have never been mentioned before. Closeness and intimacy should always be accompanied by feelings of understanding, mutual respect, trust, and a sense of security. Equally important is conscious communication. Without honest conversations, you will not reach fulfillment, which may, in consequence, contribute to moving away from each other over time.

LOVE, DESIRE, FIREWORKS... AND WHAT NEXT?

In the case of love relationships, where the intimate bond is extremely strong, feeling that we are approaching the end of the "*honeymoon*" stage and the spectacular fireworks that accompany it, it is worth summarizing this time and preparing for its consequences.

Let's stop here for a moment and consider even the simplest example: would you like to eat the same dish every day?

Serotonin, dopamine, and other chemicals that are activated in our body during falling in love do not last forever. In common sense, that high amount of hormone surges and complex processes that then take place would lead us to exhaustion if they would last all the time.

When the frenzy of passion and romantic impulses of the heart goes to the stage of a stable relationship and mature feelings, we are one step away from success to the full phase of belonging to one another.

It is important to be aware that this is a natural state that may first occur in your partner. Remember not to blame them for this state of feelings.

At this stage of the relationship, they have a chance to fully develop. Then, in our internal monologue, consent, and a great desire to spend the rest of our lives with the other half is born.

After the craziness of falling in love, there comes moments when partners make declarations that strictly result from their needs, not a temporary *"fascination of the body"*.

It is from this moment that you begin to build the path to your happiness, and the virtually unbreakable bond that has brought you together will embrace a feeling of care and security. This mutual acceptance and consent that you feel and understand gives you the opportunity to achieve common goals. Then you are 100% sure that you want to spend every free moment with yourself, because the person who is close to you has become a complement to you.

Take experience from it, plan and build a common future on the foundation of friendship, partnership, and acceptance.

Exercise

No matter if you are in a relationship or you are single, write down a list of your expectations about your partner (or future partner). Ask your partner to do the same about you. Share those lists with each other. You both may be surprised after reading them, however only by really getting to know each other, and what you openly expect from each other you will be able to create mutual and conscious agreements or you will both realize that you don't have the same approaches before getting involved in a relationship without a future.

A relationship is a place where each of us should feel safe and comfortable. However, without being convinced of the goodness and worthiness of our partner, the success of the relationship will be pointless effort for both partners.

And who likes to work long and hard without results?

Living in a happy relationship offers many possibilities. Support and mutual care translate into many successes – emotional, professional, social and family.

Each time you leave a loving home, you will attract positive people and events that will gradually add bricks to your road to happiness.

If you are felling loved and happy will be easier to smile and say a kind word to loved ones and strangers.

Let good energy carry you through life, in full acceptance of yourself and others.

IF VIOLENCE HAPPENS
IN A RELATIONSHIP

An abusive relationship is one of the most incomprehensible con-
figurations in the emotional life of two people. Its power and de-
struction make us feel constant tension, weakening mentally and
physically, eventually withdrawing from life. Often, being a victim
of psychological violence, we are not aware of it. Manipulations

to which we are subjected bear the hallmarks of violence a very thin line – what a partner can and cannot do to us.

We often live on two opposite emotional poles, once we are exceptional, irreplaceable, the most attractive, then comes the moment of the abuser's explosion, and then suddenly we become slow-witted, emotionally unbalanced, we do not deserve a happy relationship, love and respect from our partner. Nothing could be further from the truth, if in your life you have encountered veiled accusations, insults, the person closest to you threatens your decency and good intentions – please don't wait longer, leave the relationship.

However, if you are unsure whether you are a victim of violence, ask yourself a few questions:

- Does your partner humiliate you?
- Out-of-proportion jealousy as evidence that their partner did something "*wrong*" is often trying to gain control. Have you been called by your partner mentally ill?
- Whatever you do is insufficient or unsatisfactory for your partner?
- Does your partner control how often you meet with other people, like friends or family, are they jealous or possessive trying to control you? *Jealousy* has a bad reputation but it's normal to want to guard the people we love, yet out-of-proportion jealousy is the proof that they are searching for evidence that their partner did something "*wrong*" and often by that they are trying to gain control. Controlling is one of toxic behaviours you shouldn't tolerate in a relationship. Controlling behaviours may be subtle and conducted gradually, so they can be hard to

detect at first. You may even start getting used to some of them and at the end you may realize you had been hurt (boiling frog syndrome*).

- Do you feel loneliness and isolated from those close to you and disconnected from others? Loneliness is a state of mind that can be caused by life changes, poor self-esteem, mental health conditions, and personality traits.
- Is your partner trying to change their view in your eyes? It's common for people in relationships to find flaws in one another – everyone is flawed, and that's okay, but:

If your partners say, „I forbid you to do this", "You are not smart enough", "Not resourceful enough", it blocks your action, often on an emotional level. Listening to such messages makes our sense of value decrease, which in turn results in a passive attitude. We stop feeling useful, we don't engage in things with the same enthusiasm as in the past. We fade away.

Does your partner speak for you or interrupt what you say because he thinks he can do it better? Is every word you say overblown? Dominating and wanting to take control of every conversation, argument, and planning can prove fatal to you.

As a consequence, by not intervening, you will deprive yourself of the right to give your opinion, which will degrade your position in the relationship.

---

* "Boiling frog syndrome" is a metaphor used to describe the failure to act against a problematic situation which will increase in severity until reaching catastrophic proportions.

It is worth remembering that sincerity in a relationship means, apart from sharing information, also transparency against hiding it. Partners in a sincere relationship are honest and open with each other, they understand that lying will weaken the bond they share. The bond is a strong feeling of friendship, love, or shared beliefs. If you share a relationship of trust, both partners will be allowed to make mistakes. Knowing that you have the right to intimacy and privacy: you can protect your computer, and phone with passwords, but don't do it in a way that makes your partner suspicious and confused.

The topics mentioned in this chapter are difficult. However, I urge you to analyze them and reflect on your own relationship. The problem of violence, which takes many forms, is now widespread. If society is not educated on this issue, it will face emotional paralysis, which may lead to irreversible consequences. Remember that a positive relation isn't just about finding the right person, but also working to become the right person.

Take lessons from crisis situations.

Every crisis is a painful lesson, but ultimately important and necessary. It brings difficult emotions due to the number of tensions that lead to quarrels and sometimes even fights.

Importantly, even the most loving and compatible couples go through crisis times. Every day we struggle with many issues and challenges that cause us frustration, suffering or fear.

Another problem is communication, which, reduced to writing messages, often leads to understatements or misinterpretation. It is known that when in a relationship, frustrations are unloaded on the person closest to us, i.e., the partner. It is important to be aware of this state and not to build our actions on the same pattern.

A crisis in a relationship often generates a few days sometimes even a few weeks of coldness and distance. During this period, we do not feel like getting close, tender and our partner irritates us with every step. In some complicated cases, we avoid eating together, talking or spending time together. Let's allow it. Let's not add fuel to the fire. The time we spend apart will allow both parties to analyze the problem, miss each other, which will lead to an agreement and entering a different, better and higher level of the relationship.

Most crises in a relationship deepen due to the lack of openness and honest conversation, every time you deny the problem, sweeping it under the rug will not make it magically disappear. The relationship of two people is primarily a relationship of friends, bearing this in mind, we will not allow our best friend to suffer for a long time.

Invite your friend and partner for a conversation in which you show them care, support and respect, even if the crisis appeared mainly because of them. Thanks to this, you will show class and strength that will make you feel like a better person. It is worth giving a helping hand to the person first, it is worth taking the initiative to stop the conflict.

Showing tenderness and willingness to forgive your loved one will strengthen your relationship even more.

In case your crisis is prolonged and the distance that is increasing is mutual, you have two solutions:

- Couples that are unsure of their feelings, sometimes decide to break up. In time, it may turn out that it was the best decision for them. They get involved with someone new, with whom conflicts are rare or non-invasive.
- The second, noninvasive action, is the decision to ask an impartial person for help, most couples then go to a therapist.

Thanks to this solution, you have the opportunity to confront the problem, honestly confess what you really feel and where you are currently. A good therapist listens, but also mediates, directs to draw appropriate conclusions, leads to a solution to the problem, thanks to which the couple ultimately remains in a relationship.

And how is this relationship? It is often strong and unbreakable.

The first serious cracks in the relationship are a kind of test for couples, thanks to which they can practically convince themselves of the sense of their relationship. Are both sides willing and ready to make effort to maintain the relationship, rebuilding and upkeep what has been so far?

Remember that only careful listening and paying attention to your partner's gestures and reactions will lead to resolving the conflict and getting out of the crisis in which you found yourself.

**Fight for one another, because you may not meet
a person like this one more time.**

A relationship that has gone through or is going through a crisis will never be the same again. However, the fact that problems reappear, because most often they like to "*walk in pairs*", should motivate us to solve them.

The challenges that life throws at us on a daily basis, we transfer to the ground of relationships, looking for help and support in a partner. However, we often feel disappointed because we do not receive solutions at the level of our expectations from the other side.

Every disappointment leads to irritation and anger, which generate conflict, however, the need to be in a relationship is so strong that, despite unfulfilled expectations, we temper ourselves to the partner's behavior, pushing our own boundaries of what is important and needed for us.

There are no instant solutions to success in a relationship. You have to look for them within yourself. As I mentioned before, throwing responsibility on a partner, parent or therapist will not heal us. Only we, apart from our partner, have an impact on the course of our love life.

Realizing this fact, it will be easier and more transparent for us to work on it. As in the case of recovery from a disease, it is worth dividing its process into several stages:

• Work out a model of communication that will be highly conscious and understandable for both parties.

- Give yourself space for your own activities, spend some free time without your partner. Nothing brings back intimacy better than longing for it.
- Once you've developed a calm mind, start talking constructively, spend time discussing habits that could be toxic for both of you.
- In a healthy body is a healthy mind. The same is true of a relationship between two people.
- Forgive yourself for words and actions that were spoken under the influence of strong emotions.

FIRST STEP TO HEALING A RELATIONSHIP

A fulfilled relationship is one in which your inner attitude is focused on both of you. Many people like to complain that they are unlucky in love. Love is a feeling that should drive us to work on a relationship. The basic issue of building the foundation of a relationship is our autonomy in making decisions, and adjusting to our partner's choices.

This kind of balance is key to a conflict-free life. Developed empathy brings us closer to creating a good, safe relationship. Watch your other loved ones carefully, try to understand them.

The need for love and matching with a partner is one of the most important existential issues that a person must work on. In a relationship like in a mirror, our self-esteem is reflected. If we feel and let our partner feel that they are important and valuable – the whole package of relationship dependencies has a chance to cooperate with each other. How?

Treat your partner honestly and fairly. Don't treat them by your own standards and unreasonable expectations. Each of us is different, has different needs and reacts differently to situations that fate sends us. Keeping this in mind, we have a better chance of building a happy and satisfying relationship with both our partner and the environment which we are in. Often during so-called conflicts "*over nothing*" we get overly irritated, let's check the actual source of stress, our own and our partner's.

Each of us is a specialist in his field. It is important to understand and respect our division's responsibility in the relationship. It is also important to never underestimate or depreciate what the other person does in life for us.

Let me start with a simple scenario where our partner is responsible for vacuuming at home. We often do not appreciate their efforts until they stop doing it, for example, because they are ill or extremely tired. Love is a complicated relationship, delicate construction made up of many details. Do not forget about them, be grateful for them.

Reaching compromise in a relationship is an art. The trick is usually to put unnecessary emotions and resentment aside in order to reach a joint solution to the problem. The sooner we understand that the main goal is to maintain and build a happy relationship, the sooner we will start to understand the importance of compromise, which will make working out a common life strategy light, easy and pleasant.

It happens that we encounter relationships in which we can see a ruthless struggle for power. Unfortunately, all too often people like to brag that their partner "*dances to their tune.*" **Even reading this phrase, makes your skin crawl, right?!**

This attitude is a road to nowhere. Sooner or later, the dominated, oppressed partner will leave or disconnect emotionally from the relationship with their "*dictator.*" A relationship is like a passenger plane, on the way to a distant, beautiful land, but for this trip two pilots are necessary, and who complement and support each other throughout the entire length of the flight.

We often want to be attractive to others, forgetting how important it is to be attractive to our partners. After all, we spend our lives with them, they should be at the top of the list of people we want to impress.

It is known that routine creeps into life regularly, it is often the most comfortable sitting at home dressed in a tracksuit.

However, remember to break it from time to time. When you go out together into the city or even to the mall, dress in such a way that you feel attractive to each other. You will score points in the eyes of the other person, and at the same time you will raise your well-being.

The triviality and schematic nature of our everyday life mean that our passion often takes the backseat. Here it is worth looking at the issue of self-fulfillment in the field of everyday challenges.

Your satisfaction and fulfillment translate into self- confidence, and consequently, the desire to fulfill your sexual desires.

The energy and optimism that we transfer to our home life makes your loved one, proud of us and impressed, even more submissive to the "*pleasures of passion*". Let's take care of each other by sharing tenderness.

Even the smallest touch releases oxytocin in us, which is responsible for the love hormone.

Each of us, at their own pace matures to have children. Long gone are the days when, right after high school, our parents got married, which was followed by having children. Currently, parenthood is approached more consciously. Don't worry if your partner isn't ready for a baby right now. The dynamics in this matter are fast and changeable, especially in lasting relationships.

In most cases, when we start a relationship with someone, we are directly or indirectly related to their family. Let's keep in mind that every family has its secrets, intricacies and complicated construction. So, let's approach the families of our partners with care and respect. Let's not try to interfere too much in their affairs, leaving a safety buffer for them.

Each of us has a different background and it does not matter whether it is the country of birth, social or financial status. These basic issues shape us when we are young and have a strong influence on our view and perception of the world throughout our lives. So let us keep in mind what your partner's background is, listen to them carefully when they talk about their childhood. This will make it much easier for you to draw a map of the other half's personality. Creating its image, respecting it, will make the ability to navigate it resolve many conflict situations from your life.

This is somehow related to our upbringing, but also to the resourcefulness and success for which our partner worked personally without anyone's help. Treat the relationship as a partnership, where everyone brings something to it, maybe not necessarily money, but their know-how, connections, knowledge or humor. Each of you is an integral part of the relationship and a gear in the mechanism which to work depends on your dialogue and cooperation.

Each of us would like to enjoy good health for the rest of our lives. We live in times of overstimulation, often struggling with addictions, or submissive to civilization diseases. Being aware of this – be supportive to your partner, expect the same from them. *"Healthy mind in a healthy body"* – we will not escape from this cliché, because the truth flowing from it is undeniable. This unity influences how you handle stress and relate to others.

A RELATIONSHIP IS PRIMARILY A PARTNERSHIP RELATIONSHIP

Once you realize that the first step to the success of being and living in a satisfying relationship is helping your partner to be happy, as well as feeling happy, then you will be on the best path to living in complete harmony.

Every relationship, regardless of age and the level of intimacy, needs to be strengthened. Lifestyle and the so-called hygiene of life in a relationship significantly affect its quality, as well as its improvement or weakening. There is no relationship in which sooner or later routine and schematic behavior will not appear. Often your secrets or regrets that you hide deep within yourself on a daily basis come to light.

Many couples fight for a life together without caring about love. Being together for comfort, pragmatism or for the children, makes them sink into themselves as the years go by, not living the full life they dreamed of when they were young.

The foundation of any healthy relationship is an emotional bond, when you develop a mechanism of support and meeting your needs, you will be partners treating each other equally, your path to happiness will be easier and easier to implement.

Another important element that is worth working on is a successful sexual relationship. Try to be attractive for your partner, talk about their needs on a regular basis. Surprise them both in bed and out of it. Don't think of sex in terms of quantity, but quality. It would be better if the sexual encounters were less frequent, but they were a fulfillment for both you.

However, in order to climb this Mount Everest, it is important that you are people who love and respect both yourselves and others.

Exercise

Reflect on your relationship. Divide a piece of paper in 3 parts and write on the top the following questions:

1. How is your relationship now?
2. How would you like it to be?
3. What do you need to change/improve/stop doing in order to reach it?

In this case, the answers are extremely important for you, it will show you what kind of relationship you are in. Is it satisfying enough for you to plan a future together? The distance you need to travel to reach your goal and the steps you should take.

Get rid of rivalry in your relationship!

We live in times when no one wants to be dominated. Today, submission and dependence are seen as a weakness. Everyone today wants to have an influence on their life and fate. That is why it is so important that the division of roles in a relationship does not depend on stereotypical male-female archetype. Each of us is different in a million ways. We have different predispositions and talents and the more diverse they are, the better for your relationship!

It is important to complement and complete each other.

For example, when Anna fulfills the role of the household accountant, she keeps all the receipts in order and pays the bills on time, Mathew takes care of the house and fixes everything that needs to be fixed. The needs of both partners are met, their roles bring them satisfaction.

Why do couples still get into conflict? The problem arises when the partners compete with each other at all costs. After returning home, Anna tries to fix things around the house, and Mathew secretly looks through the bills and reorganizes them to his liking, for which he has no competence for. It's the worst thing they can do for themselves and their relationship. Remember life with your partner is not a competition.

When everyone wants to be on top, forcibly expand their skills while having no natural talent for them, in the end they will always feel less valuable, because they will probably never be able to achieve success equal to or surpassing the merits of their partner.

In order not to make Anna and Mathew's mistakes, it is worth remembering a few simple rules:

- Each of us is built differently, with different abilities and talents.
- There is no greater success in coexistence for a couple as when they complement each other in their roles like Yin and Yang relationship. Support your partner, motivate them to develop their own skills. Ultimately, each of you is working towards a successful relationship and a happy future together.
- Imagine that life is like a football game. Each of the players is assigned roles in which they feel and perform best for the success of the group – the team. Respect your partner's specializations, do not step their competences, they know them best. Surrender to the natural process of the game, which in this case are the next chapters of your life. At the same time, develop in your own fields and only at the pace that suits you best. Teamwork brings double benefits, at twice the rate!
- Trust your partner that when they undertake a task, they perform it at 100% of their abilities.
- It's worth watching each other, maybe it's time to change some roles previously given to each other in life? Changes are important and enriching.
- Stop blaming one another!

Example: Mathew keeps complaining that he has to be the first to take the initiative to have sex. Don't make his mistake, apparently Anna is not dominant in bed situations. Use this fact for your mutual benefit. Have fun with sex, fantasize, experiment on your own terms. Don't expect your partner to be ahead of you or on your level in everything. Would you want to be with an exact copy of yourself?!

Couples who work on their relationship more often work out compromises and psychophysical balance, they dominate other people in many aspects. This is not about financial or social success, or knowledge and wisdom in general. In their everyday functioning, the energy of coexistence – that is, living and being together for the good and the bad, makes the problems of every-day life not overwhelm them.

Furthermore, an additional life problem or random slipup triggers a domino effect. Suddenly, problems arise that you both had no idea about before. Repressed or swept away, they suddenly transform into a monster that overshadows love. The most important thing is to confront experiences, emotions, thoughts and reflections.

Living in an aura of denial, discord, constant competition and struggle for dominance generates destructive energy in which there is no room for a sense of security. The open attitude of both parties translates into countless benefits of being together, the desire to spend time together even more extensively. Joint experiences expand fields for closeness and understanding. The closeness that is created then is the currency that has the greatest value in the case of a love relationship.

Exercise

The way we handle our basic needs determines a lot of things. It is worth addressing them honestly, using your imagination or just a piece of paper and a pen.

With answers to these fundamental questions, it will be easier for us to guide our lives on the road to happiness:

- Why did you love your partner?
- What is your plan for your life one year from now?
- What are you afraid of?
- What excites you and what turns you off?
- Are you fulfilling all your fantasies? Concerning entertainment, culinary and sex?

Are you satisfied with the results of your answers? Or maybe you just found out that a few things in your life have been neglected? Read the answers again and get to work.

Don't treat your days as they are a rehearsal, life is happening here and now, live it in full of happiness and satisfaction!

TO BE AND LIVE. TOGETHER.

Loving and at the same time getting to know your other half is one of the greatest successes in life, for which we work for years.

The basis for a healthy and happy relationship is self-acceptance and self-love. The balance of love and self-acceptance leads to closeness between two people on a level that you may not have felt before. Self-love is worth learning, it is difficult and complicated for some people, but when something budges in us and we start to really like and treat ourselves with the importance that we deserve then this feeling will never fade away.

Thanks to all these components, we are able to give the other person the fullness of care, tenderness and finally love.

Every relationship requires intimacy

Closeness is one of the most delicate and intimate bonds we can establish with another human being. When this happens, we often expose ourselves completely to the other person, trusting that they will love and respect us. We hope that no knowledge of our previous life will ruin this feeling.

Intimacy equals absolute love. Without pretending, disguising ourselves and playing with appearances, we become really close to each other. Once we cross that line, we become connected. Two people meet who have their own history and pasts, made and still make mistakes, and their bodies are far from perfect. Despite all this, they love each other even more because they became intimate.

Have fun together!

It's not all work, difficult conversations, and effort. Dating is important, many couples forget how much fun it is! Going out together, during which we focus only on ourselves, brings more benefits than we can imagine. Daily routine and mundane duties take away the spontaneity and freedom of choice that is so important in the process of our relationship. Postponing spending time together, whether on short trips or holidays, inevitably distances us from each other. Sometimes I meet in my practice couples who have long forgotten why and for what they are still together.

Don't make excuses, just go on dates!

It is worth agreeing on day in the week just to spend time only with each other. For example, let it be Thursdays, which you will spend going to the cinema, a restaurant, club, where you will laugh and flirt.

And if you can't go to a restaurant, try to organize something at home, in the living room, dress nice and turn on some music, light candles, you can order food or prepare a romantic dinner yourself. Invite each other to these beautiful evenings.

Remember about one condition – during the date, do not talk about household chores, children, but focus only on each other. Then tell each other how good you look, how much you value each other, mention everything you have achieved together and what dreams you have.

Go back to the energy that you had during your first dates when there were just the two of you and the world around you seemed to not exist.

FROM THE AUTHOR'S NOTEBOOK

Completion – March 2023

Well, it's time to summarize this book…

I think that the best form to do it will be my personal explanation of what I feel love is. I have been thinking for a long time and have not come up with one clear and easy definition how to describe this basic feeling, ambiguous and at the same time so complicated.

It's like trying to capture in words a balloon that floats with the wind, or a child that follows a dog in the park. It's more or less like trying to stop falling snowflakes during a winter storm or holding a spark from a campfire.

Love through whose eyes? Mine as a therapist or as a woman, a person? As a person who often listens to strong, moving stories or their fragments from the life of the person I help to achieve emotional balance? Or maybe through the eyes of a mother, wife, daughter or friend…

I see love when I see two people opening their greatest wounds and secrets to their partner and a complete stranger to them – me, whom they decided to trust and put their faith into her to build a new path to their happiness. Then, thanks to our conversations, important issues raised, I read between the lines that there is a thread of love that connected them on their first dates. I try to lead them by this thread so that they wake up the memory of falling in love, desire that once led them to build a relationship.

The success of the three of us is the moment when during subsequent sessions, completely unconsciously, they reveal mutual love for each other. I see it and feel it while they are still insensitive, blind to what else connects them and is between them.

At such moments, sitting together in my practice I can see in their eyes, small gestures, how they want me to light the way back to themselves. They want me to bring them back to the moment when they started their dance of love, when they couldn't live without each other, when every hour, even a minute without each other was wasted time.

And I see love as the space that separates them on the sofa gets smaller as therapy progresses. During the first encounters, the space between them would fit even two angry lions. Yet they hold them tamed, meeting me and each other regularly, week after week, month after month, until suddenly anger and resentment are not invited. The space between them on the sofa disappeared, the lions are released somewhere, their recent presence is forgotten. Suddenly I see him ready to hand her a tissue, she makes sure he has a full glass of water. That's where love is. Oh yes, this is love and I am glad that it has returned tangibly and visibly!

They are already kinder to each other, show respect and tenderness to each other. She looks at him in admiration, doesn't correct him all the time, even nods her head affirmatively at what he says. During emotional moments, he gets up and hands her a handkerchief, looks at her with compassion, wanting to embrace and protect her from suffering.

All of this is love.

Love is present when they come to an agreement, in front of me as a witness, or they bring it already formulated to their home. Suddenly, it becomes normal for them to go out on their own and take initiative:

I'll stop doing this.

I'll do that more often.

I see love when, despite their differences, difficulties in communicating, different ways of growing up, very distant cultures and countries of origin, they make the effort and work on themselves individually to make decisions together. Regardless of their age and beliefs, they are still looking for ways to make it work, complement each other, and reorganize. Love is what drives them, it is the engine and motivation that drives them.

This is the beginning and the end.

They don't know it, they don't realize it, but many times I have to try really hard not to shed tears with them. Watching their excitement, regret and sincere apologies, making promises and getting back on the right path of life. I see cracks in the shell, often built up over the years, which will never miraculously disappear when we part. And no one, especially me, will guarantee that it will ever happen again.

Therapy is supposed to make people realize that systematic actions will reverse every destructive process that takes place in a couple.

And they agree not to forget, because you don't forget (it would be wonderful to be able to cut that piece of tape like when editing a movie), but yes, they are getting out of the spiral of resentment and anger into which they have fallen. Cracks such as routine, unforgivable mistakes dragging into the present, jealousy, differences of opinion and beliefs, selfishness, pride. They no longer think about what separated them. They have already made the decision to choose each other again. But this time more informed and aware of their limitations, recognizing their advantages and disadvantages, their possibilities and tools at their disposal to better their life. Keeping in mind that if they want to stay together and have a satisfying relationship, they need to work on the relationship both as a team and individually.

Sometimes, despite love, it turns out that it's not enough to stay together. They make a decision to part ways and remain on good terms. After looking deep into the relationship and themselves, they tell each other it's time to move on, but separately.

This is love too! Love for yourself. Self-love when a person picks up the remaining pieces and finds the courage to rebuild themself. This often seems impossible, but a new beginning always gives a wide range of possibilities, suddenly we can choose, improve and change – often for the better. In this is the enormity of self-love, pure only for yourself.

And this energy is contagious, giving hope to others.

So, in my search for a personal definition of love, I find that no matter how deep I search, I cannot find one. Thinking about love, I find that I don't really want to fully define it. It could mean that my search is over, that I have come to the conclusion that everything has been done. I refuse to put an end to it and put love solely as a definition. I prefer to let it manifest itself in all of its phases, to fly freely where it wants, even if it often behaves like a capricious and ill-mannered child. I don't feel competent to shape sea waves with my own hands. I prefer to continue experiencing all of this, experimenting, being a part of many stories in *which the beginning, the starter to continuing the relationship is love. Knowing for sure that loving one another is not always an easy thing, so the decision to enter a relationship should always be conscious. Considering the price that must be paid to receive the many blessings it gives us.*

And whoever is unable to pay for it, let them decide to live without love.

And whoever decides to pay for it, let them take the risk and love.

And you, what do you decide on?

Think about it.

I wish you good luck and bright light on your way.
Melissa Hernández-Jaczewska

Printed in Great Britain
by Amazon

33336402R00076